(Issued with

CAVALRY TRAINING.

INDIAN SUPPLEMENT.

Instructions in Sword Practice for Indian Cavalry.

GENERAL STAFF, INDIA,

1911.

The Naval & Military Press Ltd

Published by the
The Naval & Military Press
in association with the Royal Armouries

Unit 10 Ridgewood Industrial Park,
Uckfield, East Sussex, TN22 5QE
Tel: +44 (0) 1825 749494
Fax: +44 (0) 1825 765701

MILITARY HISTORY AT YOUR FINGERTIPS
www.naval-military-press.com

ONLINE GENEALOGY RESEARCH
www.military-genealogy.com

ONLINE MILITARY CARTOGRAPHY
www.militarymaproom.com

ROYAL ARMOURIES

The Library & Archives Department at the Royal Armouries Museum, Leeds, specialises in the history and development of armour and weapons from earliest times to the present day. Material relating to the development of artillery and modern fortifications is held at the Royal Armouries Museum, Fort Nelson.

For further information contact:
Royal Armouries Museum, Library, Armouries Drive,
Leeds, West Yorkshire LS10 1LT
Royal Armouries, Library, Fort Nelson, Down End Road, Fareham PO17 6AN

Or visit the Museum's website at
www.armouries.org.uk

In reprinting in facsimile from the original, any imperfections are inevitably reproduced and the quality may fall short of modern type and cartographic standards.
Printed and bound by CPI Antony Rowe, Eastbourne

APPENDIX I.

Instruction in the use of the sword for Indian Cavalry.

1. General principles.

The following principles should be kept in view:—

1. To attack rather than to wait an attack, and to deliver it with speed, energy and dash.

2. After parrying an attack, to immediately return with a cut or point as the circumstances permit, making every possible use of the horse.

1st stage.

The Instructor will teach the men the parts of their weapon, how to grasp it, the engage, points, cuts, and parries, from the mounted position on foot.

2nd stage.

Position as in first stage.

The Instructor will move round the men, who will point and cut to order, the Instructor showing different openings, and occasionally parrying the attacks.

APPENDIX I.

The lessons should be continued by the Instructor attacking and the men parrying. During* this stage, the Instructor will teach the Disengage, Feints, and Cutover, combining with them the attack and defence practice.

3rd stage.

As in first stage, but mounted.

4th stage.

As in second stage, but mounted, and exercises preliminary to mounted combat.

5th stage.

Mounted combat.

(i) DETAIL OF INSTRUCTION FOR THE FIRST STAGE.

Parts of the sword.—The sword is divided into two parts, hilt and blade.

The Hilt serves to protect the hand, and assists in turning an attack. It is composed of guard and grip.

The Blade is divided into two parts, " forte " (strong) and " feeble " (weak). The " forte " is that part nearer the hilt; the " feeble " that part nearer the point.

Grasp of the sword.
{ Grasp the handle with the right hand, fingers encircling the handle, thumb along the back, rear of the handle pressed well into the heel of the hand.
If preferred, in cutting the thumb may encircle the grip.

Note.—The men will be formed up round the Instructor, when the above instruction is being given.

---

*The Disengage, Feints and Cutover may be omitted in Lancer Regiments.

Photo.-Engraved & printed at the Offices of the S of I., Calcutta, 1911

ENGAGE.

Photo-Engraved & printed at the Offices of the S. of I., Calcutta, 1911

CIRCLING CUT ONE 1st POSITION.

USE OF THE SWORD FOR INDIAN CAVALRY. 3

"Fall in." — The men will form up in single rank, standing at ease, swords at the slope and without scabbards, sword knot round the wrist.

"Attention." — As usual.

"From the right, tell off by sections." — The men number off by sections, from the right of the squad.

"By sections to the front file, quick march." — No. 2 of each section advances, the remainder marking time until No. 2 has completed four paces, when No. 3 will follow and cover; then No. 1; then No. 4.

"Halt, right (or left) turn."

"Mounted position, ready." — Carry the left foot a short pace to the left, and the right foot a short pace to the right, keeping the knees straight, and the left hand by the side.

"Right prove interval." At first in two motions, and afterwards. *"judging the time".*

(1). Bring the sword smartly to the recover, that is, with the hand in line with the chin, blade perpendicular, edge to the left, elbow close to the body.

(2). Straighten the arm above the shoulder, still keeping the blade perpendicular; then, with the extended arm, lower the sword cautiously to the right, turning the edge downwards until the hand is in line with the shoulder, head and eyes directed to the right.

"Slope swords." — As usual, turning head and eyes to the front.

APPENDIX I.

"*Front prove distance.*" (At first in two motions, and afterwards "*judging the time.*")
: (1). Bring the sword smartly to the "recover."
(2). With the extended arm, lower the sword cautiously to the front, edge downwards, until the hand is in line with the shoulder, knees braced, body leaning a little forward.

"*Slope swords.*" As before.

"*Engage.*"
: Carry the point smartly to the direction of the Instructor, point as high as his breast, arm bent, elbow slightly in advance of the shoulder, elbow, hand, and forte, in line, edge of sword down.
At the same time bend both knees, and bring the left hand in front of the waist, fingers closed.

Note.—The Instructor will move round the men, making them follow him with the sword, so that it is always pointing at his breast.

The Engage against Infantry is the same, with the point lowered.

"*Point.*"
: The point will be delivered at Cavalry (or Infantry), in any direction, as follows:—
Keeping the sword and forearm in line, and pointing towards the object, straighten the arm, directing the point of the sword vigorously at the opponent, edge down.
At the same time, bend the body forward from the hips, in the direction of the point.

Note.—The Instructor will move round the squad, and direct the men to point in his direction, high or low as required.

Photo -Engraved & printed at the Offices of the S of I., Calcutta, 1911.

DIRECT CUT 1ST POSITION.

CIRCLING CUT TWO 1st POSITION.
Taken from the side to show position of the hand.

USE OF THE SWORD FOR INDIAN CAVALRY. 5

"Direct cut."
> (1) Keeping the wrist stiff, raise the arm by bending the elbow, and at the same time bring the elbow well up above the shoulder.
> (2) Still keeping the wrist stiff, cut vigorously downwards at the opponent's head, neck, or shoulders, by straightening the arm.

Note.—The Instructor will move round the squad, the men cutting in his direction as ordered.

"Circling Cut 1."
> (1) Keeping the wrist stiff, and without lowering the elbow, raise the forearm and sword vertically, and describe a circular movement with the point of the sword, (keeping the elbow as a pivot, and in front of the shoulder), upwards, backwards, and downwards, to a horizontal position to the right of the head, the arm and sword being in one line, edge to the right, and the right shoulder drawn back by turning the body from the hips.
> (2) Straighten the arm at the elbow, and deliver the cut, edge leading, with a sweep to the left, turning the body well round in the direction of the cut.
> (3) Return to "Engage."

"Circling Cut 2."
> (1) Without bending the wrist, or lowering the elbow, bend the arm at the elbow, raise the forearm and sword vertically, and describe a circular movement with the point of the sword, (keeping the elbow as a pivot), upwards, backwards, and downwards, over the left shoulder; left shoulder drawn back, and body turned from the hips.

APPENDIX I.

> The forearm and sword should be in one line, elbow in front of, and a little lower than the chin; edge of the sword to the left.
>
> (2) Straighten the arm at the elbow, and deliver the cut, edge leading, with a sweep to the right, turning the body from the hips, well round in the direction of the cut.
>
> (3) Return to the "Engage."

These cuts are invaluable as a means of developing the sword arm, giving control of the sword, and ensuring that the cuts are delivered with a true edge.

After being performed "by numbers" for a few times, they should be executed in one large, rapid, swinging movement, the correct "Engage" being assumed after each cut.

Parries.
> The parries are here described as if they were made from the "Engage" position.
>
> They should, however, be executed from any position, *e.g.*, any one parry may be executed from the final position of any other parry.
>
> In making a parry, the adversary's blade should be met with the "forte", and not with the "feeble" of one's own blade.
>
> If the parries are correctly formed as described, the adversary's blade should not only be met with the edge and forte of the blade but should finally be brought to rest by contact with the hilt. It should also be noted that the height at which the parries are made should vary, according to the height of the adversary's attack.

Photo.-Engraved & printed at the Offices of the S. of I. Calcutta, 1911

RIGHT PARRY.

Photo.-Engraved &. printed at the Offices of the S of I , Calcutta. 1911

LEFT PARRY.

USE OF THE SWORD FOR INDIAN CAVALRY.

In this way it will be seen that most of the parries practically merge into one another, and that so long as the body is protected, it does not much matter which parry is used or whether it is made higher or lower than as described.

It is always advisable to parry an attacking blade as far in front of the body as possible.

Right parry.
Straighten the arm so as to meet the attack, directing the point as far as possible towards the adversary, high or low as required, edge of the blade to the right and turned slightly upwards.

This parry protects the whole of the right side of the body.

Left parry.
Carry the sword across the body to the left to meet the adversary's attack, arm slightly bent, the blade high or low as required, edge to the left, without allowing the point to go too far from the central line. This parry protects the whole of the left side of the body.

Head parry.
Carry the sword upwards, and cover the head by the forte, blade sloping upwards, and directed to the left, edge turned upwards to meet the opposing blade. Sword hand to the right of the forehead, arm bent.

When the men have learned to form the simple parries correctly in any direction, they should be taught the circling parries.

These are formed like the simple parries, with this difference, that from the " Engage " position, before straightening the arm to meet the attack, the hand is withdrawn slightly by bending the arm at the elbow, the sword describing a small circular movement inwards and outwards. This tends to collect the opposing weapon, and in the event of an opponent making a feint and disengage attack, will take it off with much more certainty than the direct parry. The circular parries are particularly useful against attacks with the point and against all attacks by a lancer. It sometimes happens that owing to bad horsemanship, or a horse which will not face a weapon, the opponent gains the right or left rear.

In such an event the rider can only hope to ward off an attack by circling his sword vigorously from front to rear, (using the elbow as a pivot), on whichever side the attack is being made, until he can manœuvre for a position on more equal terms.

(ii) DETAIL OF INSTRUCTION FOR THE SECOND STAGE.

The man having learnt the preliminary lessons which go towards making a good swordsman, the best attacks and simplest forms of defence will now be taught, together with a few simple combinations, as explained below.

The instructor will take each man individually, both Instructor and men being dressed in masks and jackets, (gauntlets are also recommended), and armed with single sticks.

The remainder of the squad will be formed round, watching the instruction until their turn comes.

The man being brought to the "Engage", the Instructor will show an opening, and the man will immediately deliver

Photo -Engraved & printed at the Offices of the S of I , Calcutta, 1911.

HEAD PARRY.

USE OF THE SWORD FOR INDIAN CAVALRY.

a point or cut, (as ordered), which will be parried occasionally by the Instructor.

Example: The Instructor places himself on the right or left of the man, both being at the "Engage". The Instructor forms, say, Right Parry, upon which the man immediately attacks at the opening shown, (*i.e.*, at left side of Instructor) with point or cut, as ordered. This practice tends to make men quick to perceive an opening, and to attack without hesitation. As the man progresses he will be taught to parry an attack made by the Instructor, and afterwards the best "Return" from each parry. See Table—Lesson I, Parries and Returns.

When the man is proficient in this and can parry and return well, he will be taught to attack, combining with it a "disengage".

*Disengage. When two adversaries are engaged with their blades in contact in one line, and one of them carries his blade into another line, he is said to disengage. This disengage is made in order to attack on the line left open, and is made as follows :—

By a quick and close movement, detach the blade from the adversary's, carry it with a spiral motion, passing close to the hilt and arm, over, under, inside, or outside, according to the position of his blade, and deliver the point at the opening aimed at; the whole movement to be executed with great rapidity.

Example. Instructor and man engaged as before. The Instructor takes man's blade off by forming a parry. The man immediately disengages, and attacks at the opening given by

---

* *Note.*—May be omitted in Lancer Regiments.

APPENDIX I.

Instructor's parry. See Table—Lessons 2 and 3.

When the men are proficient in the above lessons the attack by feint will be taught.

*" Feints."

> The Feint is a false, or pretended, attack, made by a movement of the sword and arm, with the intention of causing the adversary to believe that a determined attack is about to be delivered, while in reality it is not so.
>
> The object of making a feint is to compel the adversary to form a parry to protect the line threatened, and so to uncover some other part of his body, thereby making an opening for the real attack.
>
> The feint should be made by inclining the body slightly, but energetically, forward and straightening the arm so as to simulate an attack with a direct point or cut. If the feint is made really well, the adversary will at once form a parry, and it is while he is forming this parry, that a point or cut should be made at the part of his body which he uncovers in trying to parry the feint.
>
> In attacking with a feint, it is important not to dwell on the feint, but, anticipating the parry the adversary will form, to attack immediately so that he may hit him on the other line while he is making the parry for the feint.

Example. Instructor and man engaged as before. The man feints at the Instructor right, left, high, or low. The Instructor endeavours to parry, upon which the man disengages and attacks in another line. See Table—Lesson 4.

---

* *Note.*—May be omitted in Lancer Regiments.

Photo.-Engraved & printed at the Offices of the S. of I., Calcutta, 1911

RIGHT PARRY LOW.

Photo.-Engraved & printed at the Offices, of the S. of I., Calcutta, 1911.

LEFT PARRY LOW.

*"Cut over"
> This cut is used when two blades are in contact and is most useful when the adversary exerts a slight pressure against the blade.
>
> It is executed as follows:—
>
> Keeping the forearm and sword in one line, bend the arm, and raise the sword so as to clear the adversary's blade by sliding the sword up it, and deliver the cut sharply downwards, edge leading, as soon as the point of the adversary's blade is clear.

TABLES OF EXAMPLES OF ATTACKS, AND PARRIES AND RETURNS.

First Lesson.—Parries and Returns.

Sword hand to Sword hand.

Man.	Instructor.	Man.	Remarks.
Forms Right Parry.	Points or cuts at opening shown.	Makes Left Parry, & returns with cut at right neck, or cheek.	No pause between Parry and Return.
Forms Left Parry	Points or cuts at opening shown.	Makes Right Parry, and returns with point at face or breast.	The Parry and Point should be done practically in one motion.
Engage Position	Cuts at head ..	Makes Head Parry and returns with circling cut at left neck or body.	
Forms right Parry	Points low ..	Makes Right Parry, low, and delivers a point at body.	

* *Note.*—May be omitted in Lancer Regiments.

APPENDIX I.

Bridle hand to bridle hand.

Man.	Instructor.	Man.	REMARKS.
Forms Right Parry.	Points or cuts at opening shown.	Makes Left Parry and returns with cut at face or neck.	
Forms Left Parry	Points or cuts at opening shown.	Makes Right Parry, and returns with point.	
Engage Position	Cuts at head ..	Makes Head Parry, & returns with cut at left neck or shoulder.	
Forms Head Parry.	Points low ..	Makes Left Circling parry, and cuts at head or shoulder.	

SECOND LESSON.* DISENGAGE ATTACKS.

Sword hand to Sword hand.

Man.	Instructor.	Man.	REMARKS.
	Takes blade off by forming Right Parry.	Disengages and points inside the arm, at breast.	
	Takes blade off by forming Left Parry.	Disengages and points outside the arm at breast.	
	Takes blade off by forming Head Parry.	Disengages and points low.	
	Takes blade off by forming Right Parry low.	Disengages and points at breast, or cuts at right arm or neck.	

Bridle hand to Bridle hand.

(As above, omitting the last example.)

* May be omitted in Lancer Regiments.

USE OF THE SWORD FOR INDIAN CAVALRY. 13

Third Lesson*—Disengages with Parries and Returns.

Sword hand to Sword hand.

Man.	Instructor.	Man.	Remarks.
Takes Instructor's blade off by forming Right Parry.	Disengages and delivers a point at breast.	Forms Left Parry and returns with cut at arm, neck, or cheek.	Practical only at a halt or walk.
Takes Instructor's blade off by forming Left Parry.	Disengages and delivers a point at breast.	Forms Right Parry and returns with point at face or breast.	Ditto.
Takes Instructor's blade off by forming Right Parry low.	Disengages and delivers a point at breast.	Forms Head Parry, and makes circling cut at left neck, or body.	Ditto.
Takes Instructor's blade off by forming Head Parry.	Disengages and delivers a point at breast.	Makes Right Parry low, and returns with point at body.	Ditto.

Bridle hand to Bridle hand.

(Repeat the first two above examples only.)

Fourth Lesson*—Feint Attacks.

Sword hand to Sword hand.

Instructor.	Man.	Remarks.
Shows opening by forming Right Parry.	Feints at opening shown, disengages, and points, or cuts outside the arm.	
Shows opening by forming Left Parry.	Feints at opening shown, disengages and points inside the arm.	

* May be omitted in Lancer Regiments.

Instructor.	Man.	Remarks.
Shows opening by forming Right Parry low.	Feints at opening shown, disengages and points, or cuts under the arm.	
Shows opening by forming Head Parry.	Feints at opening shown, disengages and delivers cut at head or shoulder.	

Bridle hand to Bridle hand.

(Repeat as above, omitting the third example.)

(iii) DETAIL OF INSTRUCTION FOR THE THIRD STAGE.

To strengthen the sword arm, and to accustom the men to deliver points and cuts on horseback, the following exercises will be performed *with the sword*.

The squad having been opened out as in the " first stage dismounted," (*i.e.*, by sections to the front file), the men will be put through the exercises of the first stage, at the "Halt."

The same exercises will then be performed at a walk, as follows :—

The squad moving round the Instructor on the "right rein," with swords at the slope, the command will be given.

"*Engage, Points at Cavalry (or Infantry), commence.*" Upon which each man will point independently in the direction of the Instructor, assuming the " Engage," after each point.

"*Steady*."—Each man will assume the " Engage " position.

"*Slope swords*."—As usual.

USE OF THE SWORD FOR INDIAN CAVALRY. 15

"*Engage*" "*Direct cuts at Cavalry (or Infantry), commence.*" { Upon which each man, in his own time, will perform the direct cut at Cavalry (or Infantry), as ordered, in the direction of the Instructor, the correct "Engage" being assumed after each cut.

"*Steady.* "—As before detailed.

"*Slope swords.*"—As usual.

"*Engage, Circling cut 1, commence.*" { Each man will perform circling cut 1 at Cavalry, in the direction of the Instructor, assuming the "Engage" after each cut.

"*Steady*" "*Circling cut 2, commence.*" { Each man will perform circling cut 2 at Cavalry, in the direction of the Instructor, returning to the "Engage," after each cut.
"*Steady*"

"*Slope swords.*"

During these exercises the Instructor will be considered the imaginary opponent, in whose direction all points and cuts will be aimed. He will therefore place himself just inside the circumference of the circle round which the men are moving which will ensure the points and cuts being delivered at him in every direction, whether to the front, flank, or rear.

The men will perform these exercises in the same order to the left, on the "left rein."

The points and cuts will subsequently be performed at the canter, until the men have sufficiently mastered their weapons to proceed to the "Fourth Stage."

The Parries are performed at the "Halt" only.

APPENDIX I.

(iv) DETAIL OF INSTRUCTION FOR THE FOURTH STAGE.

The lessons previously taught in the second stage will now be performed mounted, *with single sticks*, Instructor and men masked, and jacketted, as follows :—

The squad having been ordered to circle right at a walk, as in the previous stage, but at 3 or 4 horses' lengths distance, the Instructor will place himself within distance and will remain stationary, facing in the opposite direction to which the men are moving (Sword hand to Sword hand).

The squad will then be brought to the " Engage," and the word " attack " will be given.

As each man passes the Instructor, he will deliver an attack by point, or cut, at the various openings shown by the Instructor.

The rein being changed, the same practice will be continued to the left, the Instructor placing himself bridle hand to bridle hand.

At this period, it is important that the men should develop a good style of attack, and to ensure this they should be taught to recognise an opening immediately, and to attack thereat energetically, and without hesitation. For this reason the men will not be previously informed of the openings about to be made by the Instructor.

When some proficiency has been obtained in attacking at a walk, the men will be practised in making the simple attacks at a canter.

USE OF THE SWORD FOR INDIAN CAVALRY.

Thereafter, the Table of Lessons given in the "Second Stage dismounted," will be practised in the same manner as above.

By this time the men should have gained some proficiency in the use of the sword, and will now be practised in the following manner, first at a walk, and afterwards at a canter.

The men in pairs, facing each other at 30 yards distance, with intervals of 3 or 4 horses' lengths, will be told off as Nos. 1 and 2 ; those on one side being Nos. 1, those on the other Nos. 2.

The Instructor having detailed the attack to be made (according to the tables), the command will be given "No. 1 will attack, Walk March." Both men will move off at a walk, No. 1 will attack as detailed. No. 2 will parry and return, and both will walk on until ordered to turn about, when they will repeat the performance as they go back to their own places, and then turn about and slope swords.

Example—(See Table—Lesson 1), "No. 1 will attack, Walk March." As they move off No. 2 forms a Right Parry, No. 1 points or cuts at the opening shown, No. 2 parries the attack with Left Parry and returns with cut at neck or cheek. The order is then reversed, No. 2 attacking, and No. 1 forming the parry and return, and so on through the different Lessons of the Table.

Afterwards no particular attack will be specified, the Instructor simply giving the caution "No. 1 (or 2) will attack, Walk (or Canter) March," the men performing any form of attack previously taught.

At this period, although no particular attack is detailed, the Instructor should carefully watch each pair in turn, and correct any faults noticed.

18   APPENDIX I.

In the mounted stages, particular care must be taken to avoid hitting the horses, as the instruction detailed, while primarily applicable to training the man in the practical use of his sword, is also invaluable as a means of gradually accustoming the horse to be fearless of the blade of both rider, and opponent.

While, for this reason, the principle of not hitting the horse must be strictly adhered to in all peace training, the men must be instructed that, *in war*, a hit on the enemy's horse will be likely to make it so " out of hand " as to render the opponent helpless, and that, under such circumstances, hitting an opponent's horse is not to be avoided.

When, in this manner, some proficiency has been obtained in sword *v.* sword, dummy lances will be given to one man of each pair. The man with the lance will attack on the right or left as ordered, the swordsman performing the proper parry and return as detailed against points by the sword.

Recruits will be thoroughly trained in all four stages. The 3rd and 4th stages will be found specially useful for periodical practice by trained soldiers.

(v)—FIFTH STAGE.—PRINCIPLES OF MOUNTED COMBAT.

The object of " mounted combat " is to train the individual to an efficient use of the *Arme Blanche*, in those situations in which he may find himself placed in action, and successfully to apply to such circumstances, the broad principles of fighting learnt in " mounted combat. "

Individual combat is more likely to occur in the *Mêlée* which may take place after an attack by Cavalry on Cavalry, or on any of the other arms.

USE OF THE SWORD FOR INDIAN CAVALRY.

Individual scouts, messengers, and men on patrol, may also come upon sudden situations, in which they may have to engage in single combat, to attain their object.

In action, the natural impulse should be to ride down your man at once, with the full momentum of horse and weapon. In " mounted combat, " however, the pace must necessarily be restricted in order to avoid serious accidents, and, in this respect, the lancer is particularly handicapped in that he cannot, until at very close quarters, take full advantage of the principle vital to him, of attacking on straight lines at the gallop.

In sword *v.* sword, in meeting your opponent on the right front, if an attack be delivered with the point well to the fore, the opponent will probably endeavour to ward it off before doing anything else.

If, after the first onset, you have passed your opponent without a successful assault, you should manœuvre with a view to delivering a fresh attack on the opponent's rear. This is best carried out by turning sharply about, and avoiding wide circles.

If, after an approach, you find yourself at a standstill in close contact, then you should continue to attack vigorously and avoid acting only on the defensive. This tends to establish moral superiority. As it is likely that your opponent will also adopt the offensive, you should follow each parry with an immediate return.

In meeting your opponent on the left front, swing your horse sharply to the left, which will immediately bring you, with your sword arm free, at liberty to act on his left.

If pursued, endeavour to keep your adversary on the right rear. When attacked by more than one, you will naturally endeavour to keep them both, either to the right or left, trying to engage each in turn.

In combat against a lancer, who, to fully utilise the power of his weapon, will attack on straight lines at speed, endeavour to lure him on to circles.

In order to do this, an effective method is that of a diagonal approach, by which ground is gained to your left front (for this the " half passage " will be found most useful).

This manœuvre will probably cause the lancer to change the direction of his attack, thereby making it easier for you to ward off his point or thrust by a circling parry.

If, after the first assault, he endeavours to press on, in order to gain distance and turn about for a fresh attack, prevent this by swinging round immediately, and following him up. This may have the effect of bringing him on to a circle, where he will be at a disadvantage ; or, at any rate, it will give him no time to work up for another attack with the full momentum indispensable to his weapon.

Should you succeed in gaining a Lancer's rear, you should endeavour to gain his *left* rear, where, owing to the shortness of his reach, he is less able to damage you than if you were on his *right* rear. In the latter case, by swinging his point to the rear at the full extent of his arm, and simultaneously checking his horse, he may succeed in getting his point " home, " by your riding on to it, while still out of striking distance.

These are general principles governing " mounted combat." The points, cuts and parries taught in the previous stages are those which should be brought into play in this, the final stage of preparation for the actual combat.

G. M. Press, Simla.—No. 3 G. S. B.—10-7-11.—2,000.—J.N.B.